First Field Trips

# Farm

by Rebecca Pettiford

Bullfrog Books

# Ideas for Parents and Teachers

Bullfrog Books let children practice reading informational text at the earliest reading levels. Repetition, familiar words, and photo labels support early readers.

## Before Reading
- Discuss the cover photo. What does it tell them?
- Look at the picture glossary together. Read and discuss the words.

## Read the Book
- "Walk" through the book and look at the photos. Let the child ask questions. Point out the photo labels.
- Read the book to the child, or have him or her read independently.

## After Reading
- Prompt the child to think more. Ask: Have you ever been to a farm? Were there crops, livestock, or both?

Bullfrog Books are published by Jump!
5357 Penn Avenue South
Minneapolis, MN 55419
www.jumplibrary.com

Library of Congress Cataloging-in-Publication Data

Names: Pettiford, Rebecca, author.
Title: Farm / by Rebecca Pettiford.
Description: Minneapolis, MN: Jump!, Inc., [2016] |
Series: First field trips | Audience: Ages 5–8. |
Audience: K to grade 3. | Includes
   bibliographical references and index.
Identifiers: LCCN 2015032571 |
   ISBN 9781620312957 (hardcover: alk. paper) |
   ISBN 9781624963612 (ebook)
Subjects: LCSH: Farms—Juvenile literature. |
Domestic animals—Juvenile literature. |
School field trips—Juvenile literature.
Classification: LCC S519.P447 2016 | DDC 630—dc23
LC record available at http://lccn.loc.gov/2015032571

Editor: Jenny Fretland VanVoorst
Series Designer: Ellen Huber
Book Designer: Lindaanne Donohoe
Photo Researcher: Lindaanne Donohoe

Photo Credits: All photos by Shutterstock except:
iStock, 14, 18–19, 20–21, 22tl; Thinkstock, 5, 6–7,
8–9; Thomas Barrat/Shutterstock.com, 23tl;
Unfetteredmind/Dreamstime.com, 22br.

Printed in the United States of America at
Corporate Graphics in North Mankato, Minnesota.

# Table of Contents

# A Day at the Farm

Our class is on a field trip.

We are at a farm.

We pet animals.
Max holds a goat.
Nan feeds a horse.

Farmer Pat milks a cow.
What will he do with
the cream?

He will make butter!

Yum!

Farmer Joe
shears a sheep.

Wool comes off.

The sheep is OK.

wool

People use wool
to make clothes.

Joe's tractor makes hay.

Farm animals eat hay.

We go to the hen house.
We gather eggs.

**Will they hatch? No.**

**We will cook them.**

Pat and Joe have
a farm stand.

They sell fruits
and vegetables.

They sell eggs.

We pick out
a pumpkin.

Ben has a big one!

Our day ends with a hayride.

The farm was fun!

# Fun at the Farm

gathering eggs

petting animals

picking a pumpkin

going on a hayride

# Picture Glossary

**field trip**
A trip students take to learn about something.

**shear**
To cut the wool off a sheep.

**hatch**
To break out of an egg.

**wool**
A sheep's coat.

# Index

# To Learn More

Learning more is as easy as 1, 2, 3.

1) Go to www.factsurfer.com

2) Enter "farm" into the search box.

3) Click the "Surf" button to see a list of websites.

With factsurfer.com, finding more information is just a click away.